LIVING THINGS

ROBERT SNEDDEN

Reptiles

A⁺

Smart Apple Media

Published by Smart Apple Media
2140 Howard Drive West
North Mankato, MN 56003

Designed by Guy Callaby
Edited by Pip Morgan
Illustrations by Guy Callaby
Picture research by Su Alexander

Picture acknowledgements

Title page George McCarthy/Corbis; contents page Martin Harvey; Gallo Images/Corbis;
4 Jeff Rotman/Nature Picture Library; 5t Jeffrey L. Rotman/Corbis, b S. Blair Hedges/EPA/
Corbis; 6 Peter Blackwell/Nature Picture Library; 7t John Sullivan/Ribbit Photography, b Jeff
Rotman/Nature Picture Library; 8 Joe McDonald/Corbis; 9 Doug Perrine/Nature Picture
Library; 10 Raymond Gehman/Corbis; 11t Tony Phelps/Nature Picture Library, b John
Cancalosi/Nature Picture Library; 13t Buddy Mays/Corbis, b Doug Perrine/Nature Picture
Library; 14 Martin Harvey; Gallo Images/Corbis; 15l David A. Northcott/Corbis, r Rod
Patterson; Gallo Images/Corbis; 16 George McCarthy/Corbis; 17t Pete Oxford/Nature
Picture Library, b Frank Lane Picture Agency/Corbis; 18 Tony Heald/Nature Picture Library;
19 Tom Vezo/Nature Picture Library; 20 Conrad Maufe/Nature Picture Library; 21t Joe
McDonald/Corbis, b Peter Oxford/Nature Picture Library; 22 Joe McDonald/Corbis;
23t Dave Watts/Nature Picture Library, b Michael & Patricia Fogden/Corbis; 24 Guenther
Eichhorn (HYPERLINK "mailto:gei@cfa.harvard.edu" gei@cfa.harvard.edu); 25t Doug
Perrine/Nature Picture Library, b Anthony Bannister; Gallo Images/Corbis; 26 Adrian
Davies/Nature Picture Library; 27t Pete Oxford/Nature Picture Library, b Daniel Heuclin/
NHPA; 28 Michael & Patricia Fogden/Corbis; 29t Dr. Justin Gerlach, b Australia Zoo/
Handout/EPA/Corbis.

Front cover: Kevin Schafer/Corbis

Printed in China

Library of Congress Cataloging-in-Publication Data

Snedden, Robert.
Reptiles / by Robert Snedden.
p. cm. — (Living things)
Includes index.
ISBN-13 978-1-59920-082-8
1. Reptiles—Juvenile literature. I. Title.

QL644.2.S68 2007
597.9—dc22   2007004301

First Edition

9 8 7 6 5 4 3 2 1

Contents

What is a reptile?

What do you think of when you think of reptiles? They come in a variety of colors, shapes, and sizes, and they can look very different from one another.

Do you think of snakes and lizards as reptiles? They don't look like each other. For one thing, lizards move around on four legs, and snakes do not have legs and slither along the ground. Can both of these different types of animals be grouped together?

What about turtles and tortoises? The hard, bony shells that protect their bodies make them look different from lizards and snakes. Crocodiles and alligators, with their powerful bodies and big-toothed jaws, look like prehistoric creatures. But just like snakes, lizards, turtles, and tortoises, crocodiles and alligators are reptiles, too.

BELOW *A young saltwater crocodile lurks near the Jardine River in Australia. Fully grown, saltwater crocodiles are among the world's largest predators.*

RIGHT *These men have captured and killed an anaconda. The snake is around 20 feet (6 m) long.*

Were the dinosaurs reptiles?

Dinosaurs were a special kind of reptile. Unlike reptiles living today, dinosaurs may have been warm-blooded, which means they could get energy to warm themselves from their food. So dinosaurs were probably much more active than today's reptiles. Not all dinosaurs were giants—the smallest was about the size of a chicken.

Who's the biggest reptile?

The world's biggest lizard is the Komodo dragon of Indonesia. It can grow to more than 9.5 feet (3 m) in length and weigh more than 360 pounds (165 kg). The world's biggest snake is probably the anaconda from South America. One giant specimen was more than 36 feet (11 m) long. The reticulated python of Indonesia may be just as large. The heavyweight champion of turtles is probably the leatherback turtle—a big leatherback can weigh more than 1,500 pounds (680 kg).

The largest reptile of all is the saltwater crocodile, which lives in tropical parts of Australasia. Some individuals may measure more than 20 feet (6 m) in length and weigh one ton (0.91 t) or more, but no one has been close enough to make sure!

WOW!

The world's smallest reptiles are two lizards with long Latin names. Sphaerodactylus parthenopion *and* Sphaerodactylus ariasiae *both measure a tiny six inches (15.2 cm) long from the nose to the start of the tail.*

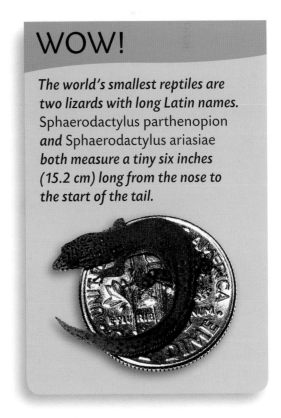

Types of reptiles

The world's reptiles can be divided into four main groups—turtles and tortoises, snakes and lizards, crocodilians, and tuataras. Each group has its own unique characteristics.

ABOVE *This leopard tortoise from Kenya is a typical member of the tortoise family. Its hard shell gives it protection against most predators.*

Turtles and tortoises

Turtles and tortoises are the only reptiles whose bodies are protected by a bony shell. Turtles live in or near water, while tortoises, which are sometimes called land turtles, live on land. Turtles and tortoises don't have teeth but they can deliver a powerful bite with their bony jaws. There are more than 200 different types of reptiles in this group.

Snakes and lizards

Most reptiles belong in this group—there are more than 5,700 different snakes and lizards in the world. Snakes and lizards might look different from each other because one has legs and the other doesn't, but they do have things in common. They have long bodies and their skin is covered in small, overlapping scales. Usually, both snakes and lizards have large mouths and tongues that are forked, or at least that have a notch in the end.

All snakes are legless, although some have tiny leg stubs near their tails. Most lizards have four legs but there are some, such as the slowworm and the Australian javelin lizard, that don't have any legs at all.

WOW!

The largest crocodile was 30 feet (12 m) long and weighed 7 tons (6.4 t). It was called Sarcosuchus imperator *and probably ate dinosaurs!*

Crocodilians

The third reptile group includes crocodiles and alligators. There are 23 different types of these powerful reptiles. They have bony plates like armor to protect the skin along their backs. They have long, powerful tails, which they use to propel themselves through water, and short legs. Also, they have strong, heavy jaws lined with pointed teeth for catching their prey.

Tuataras

The tuataras are so special, they are in a group all by themselves. These rare animals from New Zealand look very much like lizards, but are in fact a different type of reptile. They have a crest of spines running along their backs and tails. The name *tuatara* is a New Zealand Maori word meaning "peaks on the back."

ABOVE *The tuatara is a rare and unusual reptile. It is extinct on mainland New Zealand but lives on 32 small islands.*

Tuataras have unusual teeth. A single row of teeth on the lower jaw fits in between a double row on the top jaw. They are more active in cooler temperatures than other reptiles; they spend the day in their burrows, coming out at night to feed on insects and other small animals. An adult male tuatara is about 24 inches (61 cm) long.

Skin and scales

Some people believe that a snake's skin will feel slimy to the touch, but it doesn't at all. The skin of a snake, like the skin of all reptiles, is hard and dry.

Saving water

The main reason amphibians need to live near water, while reptiles do not, is their skin. The outer part of a reptile's skin is much thicker than the soft, thin skin of an amphibian; this helps reduce the loss of moisture from the reptile's body.

Many reptiles have horny scales in their skin. These are not the same as fish scales, which are bony. Reptile scales are made of a substance called keratin. This is the same substance that makes up the nails and hair of a mammal and the feathers of a bird.

RIGHT *The desert iguana lives in the Mojave and Sonoran deserts. It can stay active at temperatures of 115°F (46°C).*

Bony plates

Some reptiles have plates of bone that lie beneath the skin and give support to the scales. In tortoises and turtles, these plates connect to form a hard shell. A thin layer of skin covers the shell and a layer of thick, horny scales, called scutes, covers the skin. The scutes make up the outer shell that you see on tortoises and turtles. Softshell turtles get their name because they don't have scutes. Instead, they have a thicker layer of skin over their bony shell, which gives them a leathery look.

LEFT *The hawksbill turtle is endangered because so many have been killed for their attractive shells.*

Shedding skin

As a snake or lizard grows bigger, its scales don't grow with it. Every so often the animal sheds its old, outer skin and scales, replacing them with new skin that is growing beneath. Lizards most often shed their skin in large flakes. However, snakes usually shed their skin all in one piece. The old, upper skin layer breaks away to reveal the new layer of skin.

As they grow bigger, crocodiles, tortoises, and turtles don't shed their scales and scutes. Instead, these become thicker and larger as new layers of keratin are added underneath. However, turtles and tortoises do shed skin in flakes from their head, neck, limbs, and tail.

HOW A SNAKE SHEDS ITS SKIN

Most snakes shed their skin about six times a year. The snake uses a rough object to get the old skin off. First, it loosens the skin around its head. Gradually, as the snake slides out, the skin rolls up and turns inside out. The snake wriggles free, leaving the old skin behind.

Temperature control

Unlike birds and mammals, reptiles cannot generate heat from the food they eat to keep themselves warm. Reptiles, like amphibians, are cold-blooded and rely on the warmth of their surroundings.

Not too hot, not too cold

A reptile's body temperature increases if its surroundings are hot and it falls if they are cold. If a reptile gets too hot or too cold, its body doesn't work properly. It may not even be able to move if conditions are too extreme.

To prevent this from happening, reptiles have a number of ways of keeping their bodies at the correct temperature. One simple way is to move into the shade if it's too hot or into the sun if it's too cold. In the morning, a reptile will slowly emerge from wherever it has spent the night to warm itself in the sun. Reptiles that live in hot places, such as deserts, move back into the shade to rest during the hottest part of the day.

BELOW *Several alligators warm themselves in the sun. These captive alligators live on a ranch in Florida.*

LEFT *This sand lizard is protecting its burrow. The burrow provides shelter from predators and a place to hibernate in the winter.*

Blood and heat

Although reptiles cannot make their own heat, they can control their body warmth in another way. When you are hot, your skin flushes because the flow of blood throughout the vessels in your skin increases. Warmth from the blood is lost in the air and you cool down. Reptiles can also expand the blood vessels in their skin, but they do this so the sun can warm the blood flowing through the vessels. Reptiles want to gain heat, not lose it.

Later, in the cool evening, the blood vessels narrow so that less blood flows to the skin. This helps keep the warmth inside the reptile's body.

Cool colors

Some lizards can adjust their temperature by changing color. In the morning, they are dark in color because dark colors are better at absorbing heat. As the day goes on and they become warm enough, they grow paler in color. The light color reflects some of the sun's rays and helps prevent the lizards from becoming too warm. This is the same reason you might wear light-colored clothes in the summer and darker clothes in the winter.

ABOVE *The desert spiny lizard is an excellent climber and spends much of its time hunting in trees. A tree is also a good place to find shade from the heat of the day.*

WOW!

A reptile eats up to 50 times less than a bird or mammal of a similar size. This is because it does not need to use energy from its food to keep itself warm.

Getting around

Reptiles have a variety of ways of moving and getting from one place to another. This is not surprising when you think of all their different body shapes.

Snake movements

There are four different ways in which snakes can move.

SERPENTINE MOVEMENT

Most snakes move in a winding or twisting way called serpentine movement. The snake's muscles send wave-like movements along its body, from head to tail. As the tail pushes against the ground, it moves the snake forward. Snakes can also use serpentine movement to swim through water.

CONCERTINA MOVEMENT

Some snakes use concertina movement. The snake pulls its tail toward its head, bunching itself up like a spring or concertina. Then it moves its head forward and straightens its body.

SIDEWINDER MOVEMENT

Some desert snakes move by sidewinding. The snake moves by swinging its body sideways in loops so that it only touches the sand in two or three places. This helps the snake avoid slipping on the surface of loose sand.

CATERPILLAR MOVEMENT
(Shown from the side)

Big snakes use a caterpillar movement. Special belly scales grip the ground and pull the rest of the body along—like a caterpillar. Snakes use caterpillar movement to move through a burrow.

Striding lizards

Lizards stand with their feet spread out on either side of their bodies. As they walk, they bend their bodies from side to side so they can take bigger strides. Some lizards can stand up and run on their back legs.

Tail power

Crocodiles and alligators spend a lot of time in the water. They hold their legs close to their bodies to make themselves more streamlined and then move by swishing their powerful tails. On land, they can charge forward suddenly on their short legs, but only for a short distance.

ABOVE *The green anole is an active and nimble lizard. Special pads on its feet allow it to grip almost any surface as it runs along.*

ABOVE *The leatherback turtle's feet are large, flat flippers. They are an adaptation to a life spent mostly in water.*

Plodders and rowers

Tortoises move very slowly. They don't have any reason to go quickly. They eat plants, which don't run away, and their shells protect them from being eaten themselves. On average, a tortoise takes just one step every two seconds or so. Some turtles spend most of their time in the open ocean. A turtle uses its feet, which are flattened like flippers, to row itself through water. Turtles in the water move much faster than tortoises on land.

WOW!

The world's fastest reptile on land is the spiny-tailed iguana from Costa Rica. It can reach speeds of nearly 22 miles per hour (35 kph). In the sea, the Pacific leatherback turtle is the fastest. It can swim at 22 miles per hour (35 kph).

Seeing and hearing

The sense of sight is very important for most animals, including reptiles. Seeing is the best way reptiles can detect objects around them. Many reptiles, including some crocodiles, lizards, and tortoises, can see in color.

ABOVE *Most reptiles, such as this Nile crocodile, have excellent eyesight. The crocodile's eye is protected by a third eyelid when the animal goes underwater.*

Staring into the distance

A reptile's eye, just like yours, has a lens that focuses the light coming into the eye so objects can be seen clearly. A reptile's eyes are always set to focus on objects in the distance. If it wants to look at an object close by, it has to use muscles around its eyes to change the shape of its lens. Snakes have special muscles that push the lens forward for close vision. The lens on a camera works in the same way.

Third eye

Some lizards and the tuatara have a light detector just under the skin on the top of the head. This "third eye" can detect changes in brightness, but it can't make out shapes. It might act as a sort of light meter that helps the reptile judge how much time it has spent out in the sun.

Eyes wide open

If you have ever taken a close look at a snake, you may have noticed that it never closes its eyes. In fact, a transparent eyelid, which is actually a specialized scale, protects each of the snake's eyes. Thick scales cover the eyes of blind snakes, which spend much of their time burrowing under the ground, so they can't see at all.

Eardrum to earbone

Reptiles look as if they don't have ears, but this is because they don't have outer ear flaps like we do. Most reptiles have eardrums that are close to the surface of the skin (yours are hidden inside your ears). The reptile eardrums pick up sound vibrations as they travel on land or in water. The vibrations then pass along a small thin bone to the inner ear, which sends the sound messages to the reptile's brain. By comparison, mammals have three small bones inside their ears.

Snakes don't have eardrums and can't detect sounds traveling through the air. However, they do have a thin bone positioned between the hinge of the jaw and the inner ear. This bone picks up vibrations traveling through the ground and transmits them to the snake's inner ear.

BELOW   The king cobra, like all other snakes, does not have ears. But it can detect vibrations, such as approaching footsteps, through the ground.

LEFT   The ear of this green iguana is the small circle below and to the right of the eye. It is a small pit above the large, dark-circled scale.

Taste, smell, and heat sense

Reptiles have very keen senses of taste and smell. When it comes to hunting for food, smelling is an important way of tracking down prey. Some snakes can even track their prey by sensing its warmth.

Sometimes it is difficult to say if a reptile is tasting something or smelling it. Tasting and smelling are very similar senses. Each involves detecting tiny amounts of a substance. The difference is that you detect smells at a distance, but to taste something, you have to touch it with your tongue.

LEFT *This grass snake is exploring the smells in the air with the tips of its forked tongue.*

Tasting the air

Many reptiles don't use their tongues for tasting in the way we do. Snakes and lizards have forked tongues that constantly flicker in and out of their mouths. The tongue picks up tiny particles in the air and carries them on the tips of the tongue's fork into a pair of small holes in the snake's mouth. These holes lead to the Jacobson's organs, the reptile's scent detectors.

It is difficult to tell if the reptile is smelling or tasting what is in the air. When a snake or lizard moves its tongue in and out quickly, it means it has detected something interesting in the air.

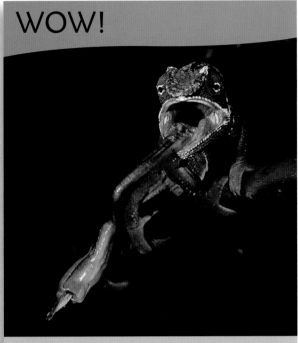

A chameleon's tongue can shoot out one and a half times the length of its body in just one tenth of a second. Inside the chameleon's mouth, the tongue folds up like a fan and is fired out by special elastic fibers like a shot from a catapult.

Yuck!

Many reptiles swallow their food whole and probably don't taste much as it goes down. However, some reptiles taste test their food before they eat it. Chameleons catch their food on the end of their long, sticky tongues. If they don't like the taste of their food, they quickly spit it out. Chameleons learn from these experiences and avoid catching nasty-tasting insects in the future.

Heat sense

Some snakes, such as pit vipers, pythons, and boas, have heat detectors in little pits on their heads. The snakes can use these to detect warmth from the animals, such as mammals and birds, that they are hunting. The detectors of a pit viper are so sensitive they can pick up changes in temperature of only a few thousandths of a degree. They can track down a mouse in its burrow on a moonless night.

BELOW *Pit vipers, such as this white-lipped viper, have heat detectors that are very sensitive to the body warmth of animals—this helps them find their prey.*

Reptile teeth

The teeth of a reptile are not like those of a mammal. Rather than having different teeth for different tasks, most reptiles have teeth that are all the same shape.

Lizard teeth

Most lizards have two rows of sharp, pointed teeth. These are usually cone-shaped and attached directly to the jawbone, rather than being in sockets like the teeth of a mammal. Some lizards that eat other animals have long teeth for gripping their prey. Often they will just grab their food and swallow it without chewing. Others have short, sharp teeth, like those on a saw blade, which they use for tearing. Plant-eating lizards often have blunt teeth.

Twisting and snapping

Crocodiles and alligators have long jaws lined with pointed teeth that they use to grab their prey. Their teeth don't have cutting edges and they can't chew. If they want to tear off pieces, they have to twist their whole bodies as they hold the prey in their jaws.

WOW!

The king cobra is the largest venomous snake in the world and can grow to 18 feet (5.5 m) in length. Its prey dies of suffocation as the poison from the cobra's bite stops its heart and lungs from working. The king cobra is also the only snake that makes a nest for its eggs.

BELOW *The jaws of the Nile crocodile are very powerful. When they snap shut, they are 30 times stronger than the jaws of a large dog.*

Bony beaks

Turtles and tortoises don't have teeth, but they do have hard, bony beaks. They bite by moving their lower jaws up and down. Like other reptiles, they don't really chew their food, but swallow it down in chunks.

LEFT *This giant tortoise enjoys a leisurely meal on Santa Cruz, one of the Galápagos Islands in the Pacific Ocean.*

Fangs and venom

All snakes have teeth for catching their prey. These teeth curve backward like hooks so the snake can pull the prey into its mouth. Some snakes produce poisonous venom to paralyze or kill their prey. The snake can then enjoy a meal that doesn't fight back.

Snakes have special teeth called fangs for delivering the venom produced by a venom gland. The fangs of some snakes have grooves called venom canals for the venom to flow down. Other snakes have fangs like hollow needles that release the venom from the tip. Snakes with long fangs can fold them back out of the way when they close their mouths.

venom

venom
canal

**INSIDE
A FANG**

venom

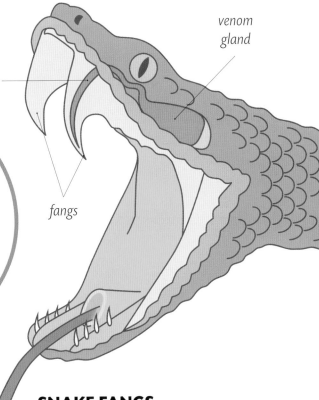

venom
gland

venom
canal

fangs

SNAKE FANGS

The fangs of a venomous snake are designed to deliver venom quickly and effectively into the prey's bloodstream.

Meal time

There are reptiles that eat plants, reptiles that are hunters, and reptiles that will eat anything they can get in their mouths.

ABOVE *Komodo dragons are powerful predators, but they are also scavengers and readily feed on dead animals.*

Lizard's lunch

Some lizards, such as iguanas, are plant-eaters, but most lizards eat insects and other small animals. Many have large sticky tongues to catch their prey—a chameleon's tongue can be as long as its body. Monitor lizards, such as the big and powerful Komodo dragon, can catch and eat small deer and pigs.

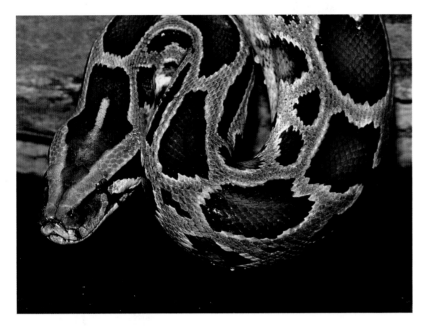

Death grip

Many nonpoisonous snakes, such as anacondas and pythons, kill their prey by suffocation. The snake wraps its muscular coils around the animal it catches and gradually tightens its grip. The pressure of the coils' grip stops the animal from breathing.

Alligator ambush

Alligators and crocodiles often lie in wait, floating very still just under the water. Only their eyes and nostrils show above the surface. When an unsuspecting animal comes to drink the water, the alligator surges forward to take it by surprise. It grabs the animal in its powerful jaws and drags it beneath the water to drown. Crocodiles and alligators also eat fish, frogs, and birds.

Turtle tidbits

Turtles and tortoises have a varied diet. Sea turtles eat seaweed, jellyfish, and small fish. Land tortoises are mostly plant-eaters, but some also eat insects and slugs. They bite off chunks with their sharp, horny beaks.

ABOVE *The Burmese python kills its prey by squeezing and suffocating it within its powerful coils.*

Open wide!

All snakes are hunters. Some, as we have seen, can poison their prey. Snakes can swallow animals that are much bigger than their heads. Their skull has extra joints that give it a very loose structure. The snake can separate the bones of its head and jaws. It can also separate its upper and lower jaws into two halves, left and right.

The two halves of the snake's lower jaw move wide apart, making the mouth much bigger. The jaws work together to pull the food in. First one side firmly holds on while the other side moves forward and grips. Then the first side releases and moves forward. Gradually the snake's food is pulled in, like hauling in a rope, hand over hand.

WOW!

The marine iguana can dive about 65 feet (20 m) into the sea in search of seaweed to eat.

Staying alive

While reptiles are busy looking for something to eat, they have to make sure they don't become prey to another animal. They have a number of ways of staying alive.

Out of sight

A good way to avoid being eaten is to avoid being seen. Some lizards and snakes are difficult to see because they are camouflaged—their colors help them blend in with their surroundings. Chameleons are known for their ability to change color, but they only use shades of green, brown, and yellow. You'll never see a red and blue spotted chameleon outside a cartoon.

Tough shells

Tortoises have their hard shells to protect them. If a tortoise is disturbed, it tucks its legs and head into the shell and sits tight until danger passes.

ABOVE *The striking green of the emerald tree boa is effective camouflage in the leafy rain forests where it lives.*

Fighting back

Many lizards stand their ground and fight if they are threatened. Some inflate their bodies with air to make themselves look bigger and make hissing sounds to warn off an attacker. If the attacker comes closer, the lizard bites, scratches, and lashes its tail. Some lizards have protective spines that make them difficult to swallow. A really big reptile like a crocodile is so powerful that any other predator would think twice before attacking it.

The end of the tail

Some lizards give up their tails to avoid losing their lives. The tail is often more brightly colored than the rest of its body and the lizard will thrash it around to draw the predator's attention. If the attacker grabs the tail it will break off, leaving the lizard to make its escape, while the predator at least gets a tail to chew on. Losing its tail doesn't do the lizard any permanent harm; the tail will grow back again. Smaller lizards regrow their tails in about a month, but big ones might take as long as a year.

Warning colors

Poisonous snakes are often brightly colored. This is a warning to other animals that it is a bad idea to try to eat them. Some snakes that are not poisonous have similar coloring to those that are. These mimics trick predators into thinking that they are poisonous, too.

ABOVE *A frilled lizard raises its large throat fans when it feels threatened. It can also charge toward its enemy on its hind legs, making itself look bigger than it is.*

WOW!

The hognose snake avoids being killed by pretending to be dead. It flips over onto its back and lets its tongue hang out of its mouth. It can also produce a foul smell intended to discourage any predator that is thinking of eating it.

A new generation

All female reptiles produce eggs from which their young will hatch. Before this happens, the eggs have to be fertilized by a male reptile. Often, males fight for the right to fertilize a female's eggs.

ABOVE *Two male lava lizards wrestle with each other for the right to mate with a female lizard.*

Look at me, look at me!

Many types of male reptiles perform displays before they mate, or fertilize the eggs. Sometimes these displays last for hours, or even longer. Male reptiles are just as interested in discouraging rival males as they are in attracting females. Some male lizards, such as fence lizards and chameleons, may change color when looking for a mate. Male anolis lizards push out flaps of colorful skin around their throats, as if they were waving a flag to attract attention.

Male and female snakes weave back and forth, twining themselves around each other, and male snakes will chase rival males away. Crocodiles growl and bellow to get a mate's attention.

LEFT *Female Olive Ridley turtles on the coast of Costa Rica leave the ocean at sunset to lay their eggs on the shore.*

Eggshells

Reptile eggs are usually fairly large and are protected by a shell. Tortoise and crocodile eggs have stiff brittle shells, while those of turtles, most lizards, and snakes have more flexible, leathery shells. Shells are important because they allow the reptile to lay its eggs on land. Amphibians have to lay their eggs in water or they will dry out.

Some female snakes and lizards don't lay their eggs at all. The thin-shelled eggs hatch inside the female's body, so she appears to give birth to live young. Reptiles that live in cooler climates, such as slowworms and adders, do this so they can keep the eggs warm inside their bodies.

Sea snakes also give birth to live young so they don't have to leave the water to lay their eggs. Reptile eggs can't be laid in water since the young reptile inside wouldn't get the oxygen it needs to survive and grow. Turtles always come out of the water to lay their eggs.

ABOVE *A green mamba snake emerges through its eggshell to take its first look at the world.*

Hatching

Young reptiles have a horny tip, called an egg tooth, on their snouts. They use this to tear a small hole in the eggshell when they are ready to hatch. After the effort of making the first opening in the shell, the young reptile often has to rest. Some pythons stay still for a few days before they continue to hatch.

Looking after baby

Young reptiles starting out in life are on their own. Most reptile eggs are abandoned and forgotten by their parents before they hatch. Only alligators and crocodiles look after their eggs and hatchlings.

BELOW *This American alligator is taking care of its young. Alligators and crocodiles are the only reptiles that take care of their offspring.*

WOW!

The temperature of an alligator's nest determines the gender of the young. If the nest is below 86°F (30°C), the eggs produce females. If it is above 93°F (34°C), the babies are all males. Temperatures in between mean both males and females will develop.

Crocodile care

All crocodilians build nests for their eggs. The nest is often a compost heap of rotting vegetation that gives off heat, keeping the eggs warm. The mother keeps a close watch on her nest and chases off any intruders. Just before they hatch, the babies make peeping calls from inside their eggs. When she hears them, their mother digs her eggs out from under the vegetation.

Once the young have hatched, the mother carefully lifts them in her powerful jaws and carries them to the river. For the next few weeks, the mother crocodile stays close by her young and quickly helps them if they get into trouble.

Turtle dash

Mother tortoises and turtles do no more for their young than try to find a safe place to lay their eggs. Many turtle eggs are uncovered and eaten by watchful birds and crabs. Those that do survive and hatch have to make a risky dash to the safety of the sea.

LEFT *Young green turtles, newly hatched from their eggs, make a dash for the ocean.*

Snaking off

Whether she lays eggs or gives birth to live young, a mother snake generally leaves the young ones to live life on their own. Some snakes, such as pythons and cobras, coil themselves around their eggs to keep the eggs warm, but they don't stay after they hatch. Some lizards also take care of their eggs—but not the hatchlings.

RIGHT *This Chinese cobra is guarding her eggs. After they hatch, the young snakes will be left to fend for themselves.*

Reptile world

Reptiles are creatures with a long history. Around 340 million years ago, they became the first animals to adapt to life on land. A number of things made this possible.

Reptiles versus amphibians

Reptiles are better equipped for life on land than amphibians. Reptiles have dry, scaly skin that prevents water loss, unlike an amphibian's smooth, thin skin that must be kept moist. Reptile eggs are protected inside a shell—amphibian eggs have to be laid in water. Reptiles have clawed feet that allow them to grip and to run—amphibians do not. Young reptiles look just like their parents; young amphibians look different and spend the first part of their lives in water.

BELOW *Snakes and other reptiles are well adapted to life on land—as this frog has discovered.*

ABOVE *The giant bronze gecko lives in the Seychelles Islands in the Indian Ocean. There may only be 3,000 of them left.*

WOW!

The earth's oldest known living animal was a giant Galápagos land tortoise called Harriet. She hatched in 1830 on one of the islands of the Galápagos in the Pacific Ocean, where she was caught by the famous naturalist Charles Darwin. Harriet died in 2006 at the Australia Zoo, where she spent the last years of her long life.

Glossary

Adaptation A feature of a living thing that makes it better suited to its particular lifestyle; the thick skin of reptiles is an adaptation to life on land.

Amphibian A type of animal, such as a frog or newt, that spends part of its life in water and part on land.

Blood vessels Networks of tubes that carry blood around the body. Arteries carry oxygen-rich blood to all parts of the body; veins carry blood to the lungs to pick up oxygen and return blood to the heart.

Camouflage Colors or patterns on an animal that make it difficult to see against its surroundings.

Cold-blooded A term that describes an animal that can't generate warmth from the food it eats; reptiles, fish, and amphibians are all cold-blooded.

Display A term that describes what a male reptile does to attract the attention of a female or to warn off a male rival.

Eardrum The part of an ear that picks up sound vibrations traveling through the air. Snakes don't have eardrums.

Extinction The term that describes the death of every member of a particular type of plant or animal. Extinction means that a living thing has ceased to exist anywhere on the earth.

Fertilize To make an egg fertile; a male reptile fertilizes the female's eggs so they can develop into young reptiles.

Flippers The broad, flat limbs of animals, such as turtles, that are specially adapted for swimming.

Hibernation A sleep-like state that some animals enter as a way of surviving harsh winter conditions. During hibernation, the animal's temperature falls and its heart and other organs work more slowly.

Jacobson's organ An organ that snakes and lizards use for detecting scents. The organ is inside the mouth.

Keratin A strong, flexible material in feathers, hair, horns, and scales.

Lens Part of the eye that focuses light so that objects can be seen clearly.

Lungs The organ that larger animals, such as amphibians, mammals, birds, and reptiles, use to take oxygen from the air they breathe.

Mate One of a pair of animals that produce young together; the pair is always male and female. Producing young is called mating.

Mimic The term that describes an animal when it takes on the appearance of something else in order to hide or protect itself.

Paralyze   To cause a person or an animal to lose its ability to move.

Predator   An animal that hunts and kills other animals (prey) for food.

Prey   An animal that is hunted and killed by another animal (predator).

Scales   Small, bony plates that overlap and protect the skin of reptiles.

Scavenger   An animal that eats other animals that are already dead, rather than hunting and killing them itself.

Scutes   The thickened, horny, or bony plates on the back of a tortoise or crocodile.

Serpentine   Appearing or moving like a snake or serpent. The winding and twisting movement that snakes use to move around.

Venom   A poisonous liquid produced by some snakes and other animals.

Web sites

www.sandiegozoo.org/animalbytes/a-reptiles.html
Information from the San Diego Zoo on a number of different types of reptiles; includes video clips.

www.biokids.umich.edu/critters/Reptilia
All about various reptiles from the University of Michigan's BioKids project; includes information on why birds might be reptiles, too!

http://animal.discovery.com/guides/atoz/snakes.html
Questions and answers on a number of reptile topics from the Animal Planet cable channel.

www.flmnh.ufl.edu/cnhc
Crocodilians—a Web site all about the natural history and conservation of crocodiles and alligators.

Index